I0480439

"Fair Use" disclaimer to inform the public that this book uses parts of copyrighted work, and uses them under the "Fair Use" act for appropriate purposes.

INTRODUCTION:

"They" (whomever "they" might happen to be) say that it takes "10,000 hours" of practicing a certain skill in order to gain "mastery" over that skill – I suppose that this idea derived from the author Malcom Gladwell – It is an interesting benchmark of achievement for a process that is otherwise unquantifiable, and I suppose that is why the idea has been debunked:

Regardless, it seems reasonable to assume that anyone that spends 10,000 hours practicing something would probably have a fairly solid grasp of the principles of that skill.

This is to say that I have a fairly solid grasp of the basic principles of "Customer Service" - You can label it by a number of different job titles – Whether a "Customer Service Agent" or a "Guest Services Representative," the skill set is all the same.

I entered the "service" field after a decade working in the "media" industry, mostly as a researcher, writer, producer and journalist – After finding the ugly business culture of the "media" industry to be not worth the attraction, I moved to the mountains of Colorado and began working at front desks of resorts and hotels – Here is a partial list:

1. The Porches of Steamboat Springs
2. The Ranch at Steamboat
3. Mountain Resorts
4. Trappeur's Crossing
5. Ski Inn
6. The Highmark
7. Holiday Inn Express
8. Quality Inn
9. Fairfield Inn & Suites
10. Wyndham Vacation Resorts
11. Hampton Inn & Suites
12. The Inn at Lost Creek
13. The Lumiere
14. Mountain Lodge at Telluride
15. The Peaks
16. Torian Plum
17. The Steamboat Grand Hotel

Additionally, once upon a time I was awarded the "Customer Service Representative of the Year Award" from the Steamboat Springs Chamber of Commerce, which I believe may have been the only year that award has ever been issued – It had been mostly in recognition for my work with the Steamboat Springs PostNet store that had achieved the fourth consecutive year as the franchise leader worldwide for sales, and my job title had been "Customer Service Manager" – Anyway, it got me a free two-night stay at a luxurious local resort as a reward, so it felt nice to see how it was "on the other side of the desk" as well!

So hopefully that is at least a worthy introduction to myself as an instructor and writer of this book concerning the skill of "Customer Service" - If you are currently working at a hotel or an auto dealership service desk or phone-bank call center or a host stand at a restaurant or just about any job in which your success as a professional depends upon your ability to successfully deliver an experience of satisfaction for your customers, then I believe that the following information in this book will be helpful for you – I have consistently achieved success for many years of working within the field of "Customer Service," and I believe that I know how to share information that you as "Agents," "Supervisors," "Managers" or "Business Owners" will want your customers to leave with smiles on their faces and return expecting the same positive experience consistently time after time – That's how we do it.

"POWER":

The idea of "power" is something that people around the world deal with differently – The different cultures of the world designate more "power" to certain individuals than to others, determined generally according to widely-accepted and mutually-shared cultural values:

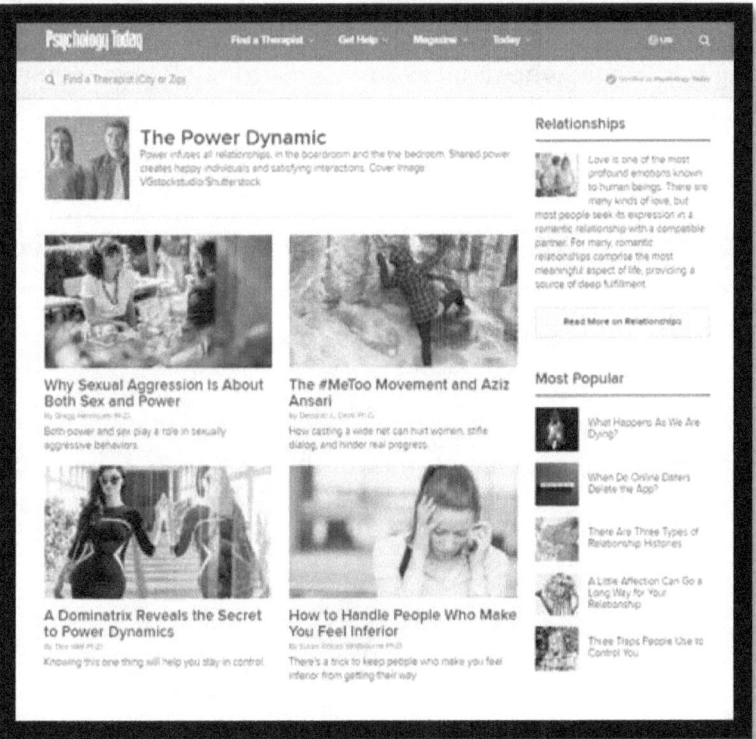

However, when we are talking about the rather specific environment of a hotel front lobby located generally anywhere within the economy of the United States, then I believe that the following description is fairly accurate to describe how the concept of "power" is understood – More specifically, the "power dynamic" between the "Guest Services Agent" and the guest:

Considering this image, who would you assume to be the individual with more "power" here?

We have a smiling customer facing an apparently helpful "Customer Service Representative" of some kind – Perhaps this would be a "Retail Associate" helping a customer with a purchase.

So who has "the power?" The customer or the associate? Think about it with consideration for "the golden rule"... which is, "He who has the most gold makes the rules!"

Yep... You may not like it... I may not like it...But that's only because we don't have the "gold," if you understand my meaning – However, those who do have the "gold" most often had to answer to someone else with the "gold" first before they had their own "gold" - So that is what you are doing now – I believe that the skills found in this book will help you earn more "gold," more promotions, more gratuities and more job satisfaction for yourself as well.

So when we acknowledge that within a customer service power dynamic between two individuals, the one with the "gold" makes the rules and has the "power" which leads to the following concept that is fundamentally essential in order to firmly grasp, understand, and ultimately master the skill of "Customer Service" – Remember this word and tattoo it into your brain – "RESPECT."

We have respect for our customers, clients and guests – There is a reason why you, as a "Customer Service Agent," are answering the phone call from the "customer" - Because YOU are there for THEM, and you are getting paid to be there for THEM – Ultimately, in plain language, YOU ARE THERE TO *SERVE* THEM! Deal with it, or get a different job.

Does that send a ripple of anger and humiliation through your heart, your soul and your mind? Fret not – It is going to be okay – I will guide you through this, and it is not scary – There is a second fundamental concept that you MUST not only "understand," but completely master in order to achieve any success at all within the "service" industry – That fundamental word is "HUMILITY."

(If your role model looks like this, then the "service" industry is not for you)

Now here is an unexpected twist...

"The word hospitality comes from the Latin hospes, which came from the word hostis, which originally meant 'to have power.'"

Well now isn't that interesting? The meaning of the origin of the word "hospitality" is "to have power" - So what could this mean for someone working in the "hospitality" industry?

If you think about it a little more... Considering that the word "hospitality" ultimately means "to have power"... So who has the "power?" The individual that has the "power" to sell a hotel room, or the individual who has the "power" to rent a hotel room for a night?

I would say that to a "travelling salesman" driving late at night through a town with almost no hotel vacancy during a torrential rainstorm, that the individual with the ability to rent a hotel room would ultimately be the one in "power," right? Yes or no?

If the "Guest Services Agent" gives the unfortunate "travelling salesman" a crabby attitude, that salesman can pull out his smart phone right there in the hotel lobby and write a damaging review for the rude behavior of the "Guest Services Agent"... So now this is so confusing... Who has the "power?"

"Yīnyáng"

The concept of "yin and yang" ("yīnyáng") is an ancient Taoist philosophy that is both very simple and also very complex – The simple part is that there are two parts... One called "yin" and one called "yang," like a never-ending story between only two characters.

Anyway, this isn't a book about "spirituality," as there are plenty of other books for that, however the basic philosophical principle of the balance between two opposites is the concept that I wish to reference - "Yin" needs "yang," and "yang" needs "yin" (Incidentally, "yin" is the word for the "female principle," and "yang" is the word for the "male principle," in a similar why that "gender" is used in Latin languages).

A guest needs a "Guest Services Agent," and a "Guest Services Agent" needs guests – So who is in power? Well... now we know a little more about the factors involved, don't we? So, I'll ask the question one last time and I am confident that you now know the answer – Who has the power? "He who has the most gold makes the rules"... (wink)... If you "get it," then you are getting it.

SALESMANSHIP:

Many people choose to enter the field of "hospitality" and other service-oriented professions for many different reasons, however there do appear to be a handful of reasons that someone would consider entering this field instead of another profession, such as "equity-stock management" or "mercenary soldier" - There are many, many other types of jobs available – Why "service?"

In my personal case, I entered the "service" field because I was burned-out from the high-pressure "sales" industry as the "sales quota" goals seemed to increase even as I achieved each increasing level, like a dog chasing a fake rabbit around a race track... exactly.

However, as I began working in "service" roles after my rigorous "sales" experience, I realized that many of the skills that I had honed within the kiln furnace of commission sales had become suddenly very useful for "selling" the crumb-cakes out of some "customer service" - Truly, customers were blown away – Many of them were visibly shocked – I was chuckling to myself... I was making about 100 times the sales as a "Service Associate" than I had as a "Salesman"... Because I never had to make one single "cold call"... The customers were streaming in through the door on their own like lambs directly into a lion's den... And I devoured them... And they loved it so much they returned over and over again!

So, what is the difference between "service" and "sales?" It is pretty simple to explain, but can be rather challenging to master:

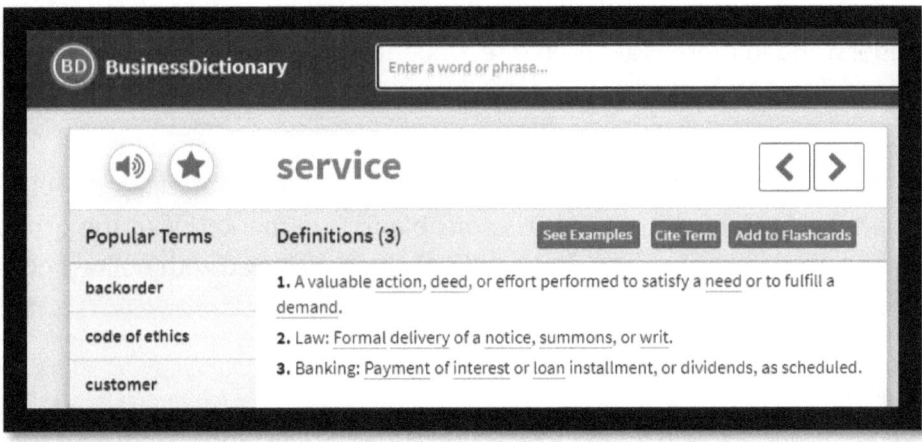

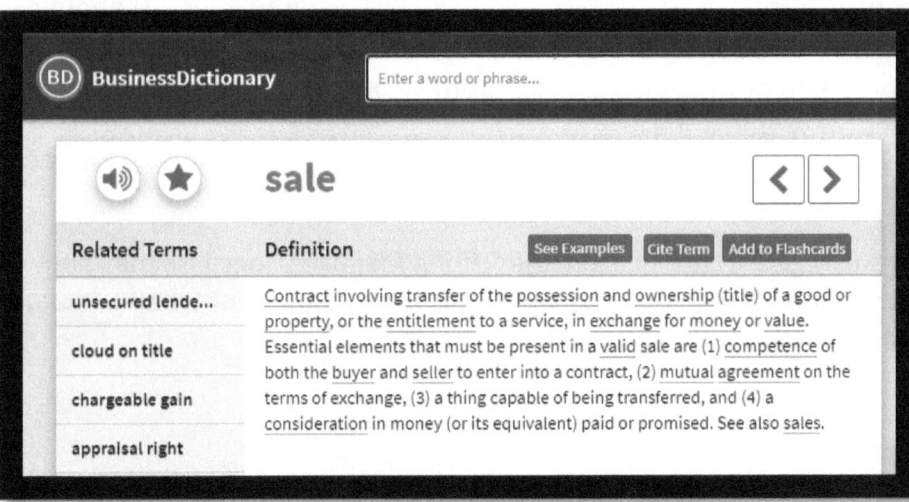

By my definition, a "sale" is the agreement that the customer will "buy" something, and "service" is the "maintenance" of a "sale."

As you may have already recognized as a reader of this book, many of the concepts that I will share with you have a few different ways of looking at it.

In a similar way that the balance of "power" in a "customer service" setting can be understood with nuance in different ways, also the concept of "sales" can also be understood in more ways than one, depending upon individual circumstances.

For example, as a "Guest Services Agent" at a 4-star rated hotel, I can feel somewhat grateful that I was not responsible for the marketing of the property in order to lure potential guests, but need only be concerned with politely collecting the money for the sale.

However, there are also multiple interpretations of the word "sale" - One way that I have been almost 100% certain that I will be hired after just about every interview for a "Front Desk Agent" hotel position is that I have my own interpretation of what I am "selling" at the front desk – I am "selling" them walking away with a smile!

This usually gets a chuckle from the "Hiring Manager," because they know all too well what it is like when guests walk away from a hotel front desk *without* smiles on their faces... And it ain't good.

So, therefore, what would the guest be "buying" from a "Guest Services Agent" if the guest already purchased the hotel reservation? They are "buying" a smile from you – You give it to them, and they walk away with it – Get it?

Yeah – You got it – So the guest approaches the front desk – You smile at the guest and make the guest's life as easy as humanly possible (this involves knowing how to do your job, so make sure that you know how to do your job) - The guest already knows how much the room will cost, and all the guest wants to do is have a pleasant interaction during the necessary "payment" phase of the sale of the reservation, and the guest wants to move along and go about taking care of business... But with a little better attitude than before checking in to the hotel, right? And that is what you sell – You get "paid" by your paycheck as well as with gratuities and positive reviews online.

So how do we do this? As with just about all of the material in this book, the "answers" are simple... However, the "execution" can be challenging.

The easiest way to do this is to do what you would wish that a "Guest Services Agent" would do if you were the guest yourself – Now we are *really* talking about "The Golden Rule" - "Do unto others that which you would wish others do unto you" - What would you want to see? Someone with a wrinkled shirt, a mouth full of corn chips, staring at a smart phone and telling you, "There is nothing that I can do for you?"

No, you would not look forward to an interaction with such an individual – Alternatively, how would you like to walk into a hotel lobby and be greeted by a "Guest Services Agent" with a cheerful smile and attentive to making sure that your reservation details are correct and that the check-in process is as efficient and pleasant as possible?

Yes, this is what you would look forward to as a guest checking into a hotel – So, you know, do it that way – And if you don't, then immediately accept accountability, apologize, and tell the guest that you will do everything possible to take care of any problem or clarify any confusion... The first magic phrase is...

"RESOLVING THIS ISSUE IS AS IMPORTANT TO ME AS IT IS TO YOU."

I suggest that you go ahead and just say this out loud a few times to get your mouth muscles accustomed to this phrase that you will undoubtedly say several times per day if you choose to work in the role of "Guest Services Agent" - You can take it to the bank - And here is the other one...

"THE CAUSE OF THIS ISSUE MAY NOT BE MY 'FAULT,'

BUT RESOLVING THIS ISSUE IS MY 'RESPONSIBILITY.'"

And then I would recommend saying this phrase over and over again out loud as well – These are two magical phrases that will save you almost every time – This is expressing that you have respect for the guest and that you are acting in the role of a professional and that you take their business with the company very seriously – Yes, even though "Guest Services" can be one of the most fun jobs in the world, it can also be quite a serious job as well.

If you assure the guest that resolving the issue is as important to you as it is to the guest, then you are setting them at ease that you "get it" and that they do not need to "micro-manage" the situation because they will feel that they can trust you... Until you mess up, that is... So, make sure that you know how to do your job – Guests are not looking for a contest or a "training opportunity," they just want to stay at your hotel without any hassles – If you assure them that taking care of the hassles is your job, then they can enjoy a cup of coffee in the lobby and give you the space to do your job – Again, say these two magical phrases out loud – Most certainly your supervisor will be impressed and you will make just about every "sale" with each happy guest walking away wearing a recently-purchased smile.

EXPECTATIONS:

Have you ever heard of the term "managed expectations" before? I am sure that you can figure out the concept pretty easily... "managing" the "expectations" of someone, right?

How would we appropriately manage the expectations of a family of guests that had not arrived by 11:00 pm, and they had not yet called to cancel their reservation? Additionally, there had been white-out snow conditions on the highway and just before you were about to hand your shift over to the "Night Auditor," you noticed that the "family" had been booked into a single room with a king bed – What would you do?

Seriously, think about it.

Would you think, "Not my problem, and I have a freshly-packed bowl waiting for me at home and I want to get out of here," or would you think, "Uh-oh, I had better make a record of this confusion with the reservation into the front-desk log, and to be sure to clearly explain the problem to the Night Auditor – Just before I leave to go home, I will try to call the family's cell phone number on file and at least leave a message that we will do everything that we can to accommodate them."

That sounds like the thoughts of a pretty seasoned "service" professional, wouldn't you say? With this approach to customer service, you are managing the expectations of your guests.

When they finally arrive to the hotel after driving through a blizzard, the family will already know about the situation before they enter the front lobby and they will not be faced with the shock of the bad news only after arriving to the front desk – This gives the "decision maker" of the family time to independently fume and vent frustration prior to arriving in front of you.

Additionally, this gives both you and your guests time to prepare some possible alternatives, perhaps even including a discounted or complimentary stay, depending on the policy established by your management – By greeting your guests prepared with alternatives, this will greatly help to diffuse the conflict.

So you can apply that same set of principles to just about any upcoming conflict – Manage the expectations of your guests in order to protect yourself from a terrifying escalation that could result in a guest having an angry meltdown in the public view of your hotel front lobby – Another common way to think about this is "nipping it in the bud," if ya' know what I mean... And I'm not talking about your packed glass again, sheesh! 🙂

OVER-DELIVERY IS EASIER (& BETTER):

Haven't we all heard that "there is no easy way?" I disagree, and in fact, I believe that "the easy way" is actually the vastly better way to provide exceptional customer service.

What is "the easy way?" For one thing, it is mostly this... DOING IT CORRECTLY THE FIRST TIME.

In order to be most assured of "doing it correctly the first time," it is essential to _pay attention_ to what you are doing, which most often means paying attention to what your customer is saying – It may sound simple, however I have noticed from many years of experience working in this industry that many people are so poor that they can't even afford to "pay attention"... I think you got it, right?

But, in actuality, they really were "poor"... They were very "poor" at doing their jobs, they were very "poor" at providing customer service, and therefore they were also very financially "poor" because they could never seem to get out of their own way and simply focus their attention upon someone other than themselves for a brief moment of time... When that was what they were being paid to do... And not doing it... A lot of them... I have pretty much seen it all, and I've seen a lot of dead weight clock-watching through work shifts sleepwalking from one paycheck to the next... That's not only no way to work, that's no way to live!

NOBODY IS RIGHT, EVERYBODY IS WRONG,

& IT DOESN'T MATTER:

Why does it seem to be so important to so many people that they be proven "right?" People will devolve into physical violence just to "prove a point" - It really is crazy behavior – It really does not achieve anything worthwhile – Punching someone in the face will not force anybody to agree that you are "right" and they are "wrong" unless you kneel on their chest like a bully on a playground calling for "Uncle!"

But it happens – We all know that it happens all the time – It appears to be an unavoidable characteristic of basic human nature, and when you are working at the front desk of a hotel in the role of "Guest Services Agent," you are on the "front lines" of interaction with the guests of the hotel - "The buck stops here" means that you have to deal with everything from clogged toilets to potentially domestic violence situations – No matter what, in the heat of a conflict with a guest, remember this – The guest is always "right" at the time that you are interacting with them – Otherwise, attempting to "prove them wrong" will do nothing more than escalate the rage being projected in your direction.

At the same time, it is not a good idea to say to a guest words similar to this, "Yes, this is my fault and I accept responsibility for it" - Not so fast – Sheraton Hotels used to refund guests for the cost of their stay if they complained about *anything* – Yes, that policy was abused and the company ended the promotion – Guests will try to get away with stuff, so you also don't want to "give away the farm" - Your management staff will have a policy to follow, however a complete refund for a night's stay is typically too far to go unless it was a very serious issue.

Therefore, I suggest adding the following phrase to your repertoire:

"I am very sorry for this confusion and for your frustration – I will take care of this issue immediately and follow up with you shortly to let you know what we will be able to do for you – Would you like me to call your cell phone number?"

Something similar to that – You can find some verbiage that fits your style – However, it is very helpful to use the word "we," and not "I," when responding to a guest complaint since you represent the full staff of the hotel front desk including the "Front Desk Manager," so try to make it clear that you share responsibility as a "team," and especially when you *know* for sure that the issue was not your fault... However, it is your _____. (Fill in the blank – This is the one quiz at the end of the lesson – Congratulations, you completed the course!)

"A man without a smiling face must not open a shop."

— Chinese Proverb